SPAIN

Madeline Donaldson

Lerner Publications Company • Minneapolis

For Mrs. Sherman, my first mentor

Lerner Publications Company
A division of Lerner Publishing Group, Inc.
241 First Avenue North
Minneapolis, MN 55401 U.S.A.

Website address: www.lernerbooks.com

Library of Congress Cataloging-in-Publication Data

Donaldson, Madeline.
    Spain / by Madeline Donaldson.
      p.   cm. — (Country explorers)
    Includes index.
    ISBN 978–0–7613–6410–8 (lib. bdg. : alk. paper)
    1. Spain—Juvenile literature. I. Title.
DP17.D66 2012
946—dc22   2010048610

Manufactured in the United States of America
1 — MG — 7/15/11

Table of Contents

Welcome!

You've come to Spain! This country is in southwestern Europe. To the northeast are France and the tiny nation of Andorra. Spain shares a long western border with Portugal. The Atlantic Ocean touches Spain's northwestern and southwestern coasts. The Mediterranean Sea lies to the east and south.

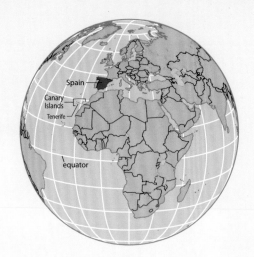

Other Parts of Spain

Spain also includes islands and cities. The Balearic Islands lie in the Mediterranean Sea. The Canary Islands sit to the southwest in the Atlantic Ocean. Ceuta and Melilla are Spanish cities on the northern coast of Africa.

The Spanish coast of the Mediterranean Sea has many beautiful beaches.

Many Parts

Many regions make up Spain. Some regions were kingdoms long ago. Navarra, Aragon, and Catalonia are in the north. Valencia is to the east, and Andalusia is in the south.

The ruins of ancient kingdoms can be seen in many of Spain's regions. This one is in Aragon.

The Meseta is a huge plateau (a high, flat area). It covers central Spain. It was once the kingdom of Castilla y Leon. Mountains break up the high flatland. Madrid is the capital of Spain. It lies in this region.

The Meseta is a plateau that covers central Spain.

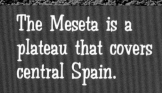

Lots of Mountains

Mountains can be found throughout Spain. The Cantabrian range lies in the northwest. The tall Pyrenees separate France and Spain in the northeast. These ranges get snow in winter.

This scenic town sits at the base of the Pyrenees in northern Spain.

The word *sierra* means "mountain range." The Sierra de Guadarrama and the Sierra Morena rise from the Meseta. In the south sits the Sierra Nevada. Mainland Spain's tallest point—Mulhacen—rises within this range.

Mount Teide is the tallest mountain in Spain.

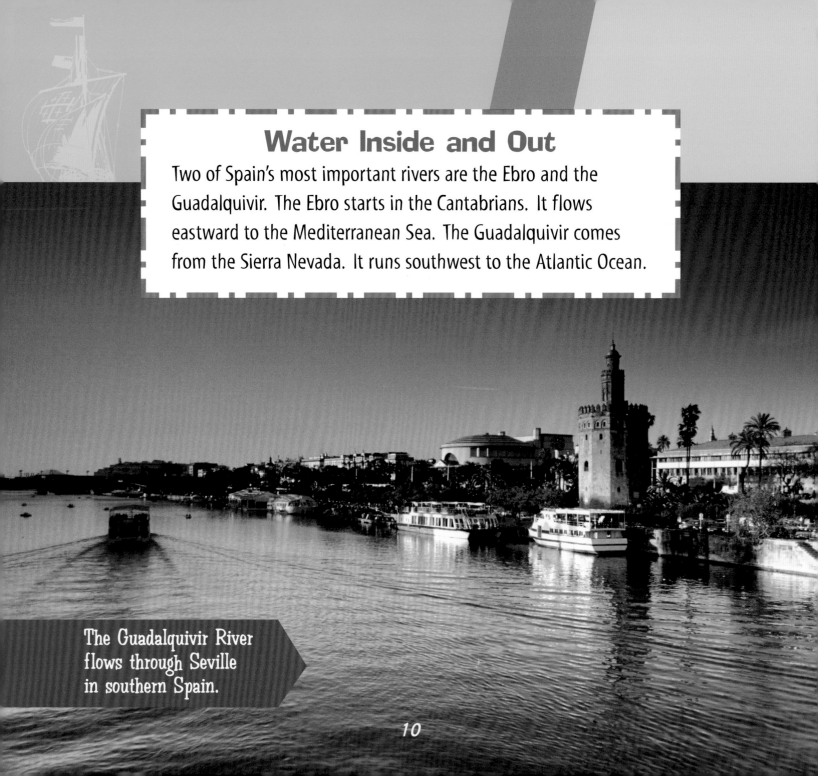

Water Inside and Out

Two of Spain's most important rivers are the Ebro and the Guadalquivir. The Ebro starts in the Cantabrians. It flows eastward to the Mediterranean Sea. The Guadalquivir comes from the Sierra Nevada. It runs southwest to the Atlantic Ocean.

The Guadalquivir River flows through Seville in southern Spain.

Goods and people travel to and from Spain by water. Port cities dot the country's coastlines. The largest port, Bilbao, sits on the Atlantic.

Bilbao is a port on the northern coast of Spain.

Central Spain

The Meseta forms the largest region in Spain. This plateau is hot and dry in the summer. Winters are cold, but snow is rare. Farming is hard in this area. Crops that can grow there include grains, olives, and saffron. Sheep graze on local grasses.

A worker reveals the spikes of a crocus flower. These spikes are used to make saffron.

Saffron

Saffron is a bright yellow spice. It is made from the spiky parts of the crocus flower. Each flower has only three spikes. So it takes thousands of crocuses to make just a little bit of saffron.

Madrid, Toledo, and Segovia sit in the center of the Meseta. Many people live in these cities. But the rest of the region has fewer people.

Madrid is the largest city in Spain. It is home to more than three million people.

13

Coastal Spain

Narrow plains line Spain's Mediterranean coast. The plains have a mild climate throughout the year. Farmers can grow olives and grapes. Beautiful, white-sand beaches attract visitors.

The Mediterranean coast is a popular place for growing grapes.

The coast of northern Spain gets the most rain. Temperatures there don't get very hot or cold. In the city of La Coruna, temperatures average 66°F (19°C) in July. In January, temperatures there drop only to about 51°F (11°C).

Gibraltar

Gibraltar lies in southern Spain. The area is a thin strip of land surrounded by water. This rocky spot belongs to Great Britain.

La Coruna is one of the largest cities in northwestern Spain.

Long Ago in Spain

People have been living in Spain for thousands of years. The area was once home to ancient Phoenicians, Greeks, and Romans.

The Romans built this aqueduct in central Spain more than eighteen hundred years ago. An aqueduct carries water from one place to another.

In the 700s, Arabs from Africa took over most of central and southern Spain. These Arabs were known as Moors. They ruled for about five hundred years. The Moors built large palaces called alcazars. They are still standing.

The Alcazar Palace in Seville contains many richly decorated rooms and this courtyard.

From Many Kingdoms to One

The kingdoms of Aragon, Catalonia, Valencia, and Castilla y Leon surrounded the part of Spain that the Moors controlled. These kingdoms tried to free Spain from Moorish rule. By the mid-1200s, they had succeeded!

This illustration shows three Spanish kings defeating the Moors in 1212.

Spain was still a land of many kingdoms. But by the 1500s, these kingdoms had united into one. The kings and queens of the large kingdom also ruled other faraway lands. Spain controlled parts of Asia, North America, the Caribbean, Central America, and South America.

Christopher Columbus

Christopher Columbus was an explorer. In the late 1400s, the Spanish king and queen paid for Columbus's exploring trips. His ships landed on islands in the Caribbean Sea. These trips helped Spain claim lands in the Caribbean and beyond.

This illustration shows Christopher Columbus telling the Spanish court of his exploration in the Caribbean.

Modern Spain

Spain went through tough times in the 1900s. War forced the Spanish king to leave. Francisco Franco took power. He had total control from 1939 to 1975. Franco died in 1975. By then, Spain had a king again. Spain would also have a lawmaking body.

Francisco Franco *(front center)* salutes thousands of troops in a victory parade in 1939.

Juan Carlos I became king in 1975. He doesn't actually run the country. His role is mostly ceremonial. But his support means a lot to Spanish leaders.

King Juan Carlos I waves to a crowd outside of a palace in Madrid in 2011.

These Valencian children are wearing historical clothing for a festival.

Who Are the Spaniards?

Most people who live in Spain are Spanish. But Spaniards have close regional ties too. They may call themselves Castilians, Valencians, Basques, or Catalans.

Spain is also home to about two hundred thousand Gitanos. They share ties with Gypsies who roamed Europe in earlier times. Newcomers from South America, Morocco, Romania, and Britain have come to live and work in Spain.

Basque people live on the western edge of the Pyrenees. These men are performing a traditional Basque dance.

23

Spain's Language

Castilian Spanish is the country's official language. People spoke this language in the old kingdom of Castilla y Leon. Many still do. People in Catalonia, Galicia, the Basque Country, and other parts of Spain also have their own regional languages.

Spaniards enjoy getting together at a public square in Castilla y Leon.

People living in many countries that Spain used to rule speak Spanish. In fact, more people outside of Spain than inside of Spain speak Spanish.

The voting sign below is written in both Catalan, the language of Catalonia, and Castilian Spanish.

COL·LEGI ELECTORAL
COLEGIO ELECTORAL

5-65-U 5-66-U 5-67-U
5-68-U 5-69-U 5-70-U

DISTRICTE
DISTRITO

Telèfon d'informació electoral | Teléfono de información electoral
901.101.900

SECCIONS
SECCIONES

Religion and Holidays

Most Spaniards are Roman Catholics.
They celebrate Christmas, Easter, and
other Christian holidays. Madrid's New
Year celebrations attract thousands
of people.

Fireworks explode over the Madrid
skyline for its New Year celebration.

Regional holidays often bring the most excitement. They honor saints who are important to the region. People wear historical clothing. Fireworks, parades, music, and bullfights may be part of the celebrations.

Dear Aunt Mary,
It's May 15, and we're in Madrid. This day is the start of a holiday that honors San Isidro. He's an important saint in the city. We've heard that the country's best bullfighters perform in Las Ventas bullring for the holiday. We're hoping to get tickets. The bullfights stretch over twenty days!
See you soon.
Sally

Las Ventas bullring, Madrid

Family Life

Spanish families are close. Children feel the love of all family members. Grown children may live with their parents until they marry.

Many families enjoy playing and listening to music together.

Spanish families love to get together. Some visits last for hours! Guests might bring a dessert or flowers. Hosts serve coffee and light snacks. Talking is required!

Two Last Names

Spanish kids have two official last names. The first one is from their father. The second one is from their mother. For example, the full name of Spanish actress Penelope Cruz is Penelope Cruz Sanchez.

Spanish hosts often entertain outdoors. Many generations will get together.

Spanish Cities

Nearly four out of five Spaniards live in cities. Many cities line the coasts. Barcelona, Valencia, Malaga, and Cadiz are important port cities. Madrid, Seville, and Saragossa are big inland cities.

Barcelona is the second-biggest city in Spain.

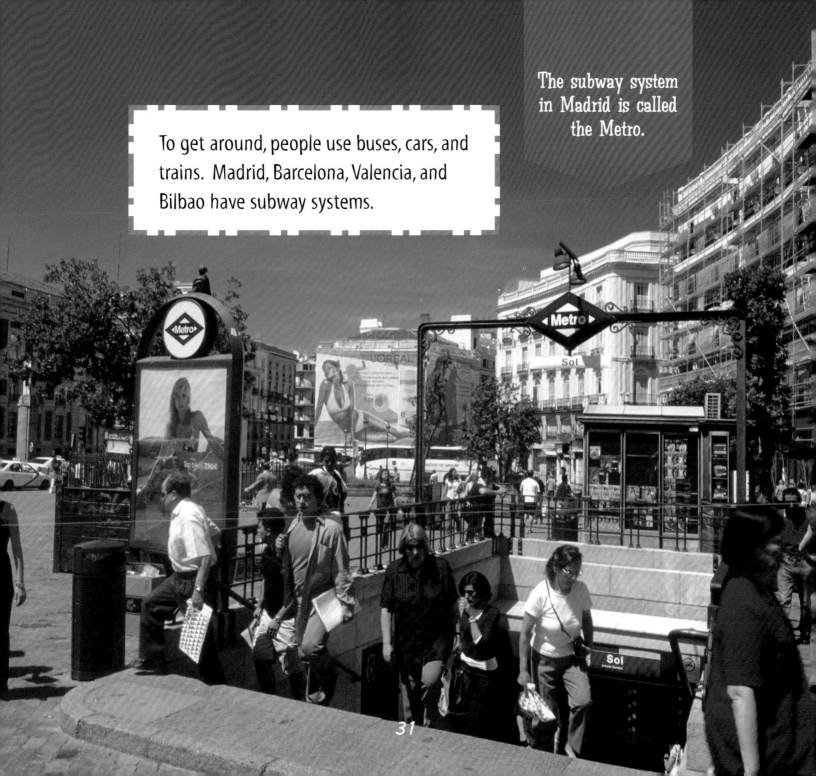

To get around, people use buses, cars, and trains. Madrid, Barcelona, Valencia, and Bilbao have subway systems.

The subway system in Madrid is called the Metro.

31

Country Life

Only one out of five Spaniards lives in the countryside.
Homes and shops in Spanish villages are packed together.

This village in northern Spain is tightly packed on a mountaintop.

Spaniards who live in the country often farm the land.
They may live in a small town and travel to and from the farm.
Or they may live in a house right on the farm.

This man is harvesting grapes at a vineyard in northeastern Spain.

Let's Eat!

Spaniards love fresh food. Cooks shop at outdoor markets almost every day. They often buy fish, pork, beans, and vegetables. Garlic, olive oil, paprika, saffron, and peppers spice most dishes. Rice and bread are popular side dishes.

This outdoor market is in Barcelona.

Families try to eat at least one meal a day together. They usually eat a big lunch between one thirty and three thirty. Dinner is a lighter meal served anytime after eight in the evening.

Yea for Churros!

A Spanish kid might eat churros for breakfast. Churros are thick strands of dough that are deep-fried in olive oil. Then they're brushed with sugar. Yum!

Lunch is an important meal for Spanish families.

35

The Arts

Spanish flamenco blends singing, dancing, and guitar playing. The singers sing with a lot of feeling. The dancing has fancy footwork. The guitar ties the two together.

Modern Spanish singers have brought their music to people far beyond Spain's borders. Pop star Enrique Iglesias and rapper Maria Rodriguez are well-known stars around the world.

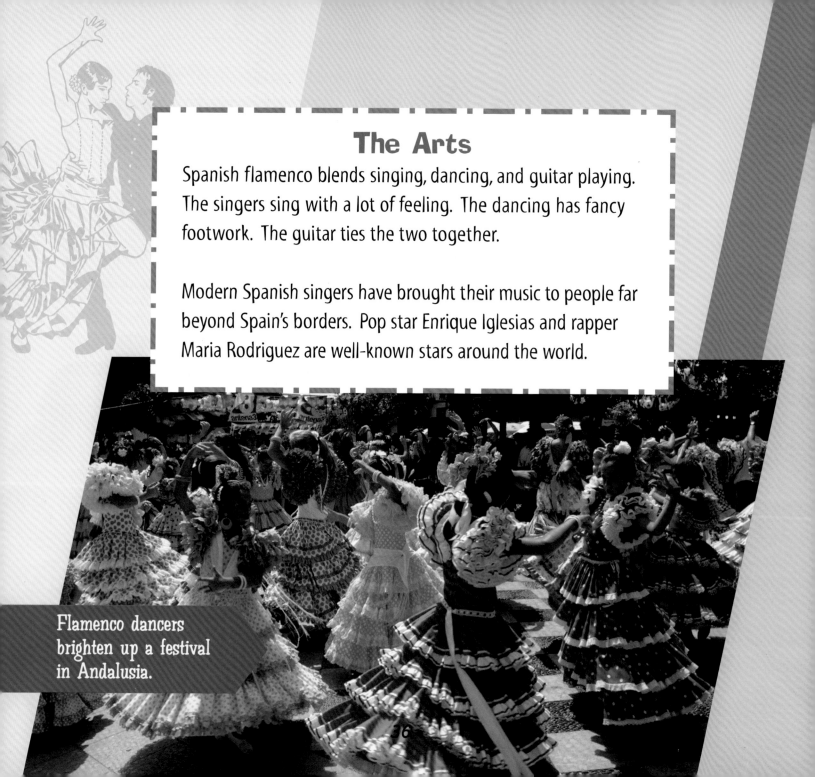

Flamenco dancers brighten up a festival in Andalusia.

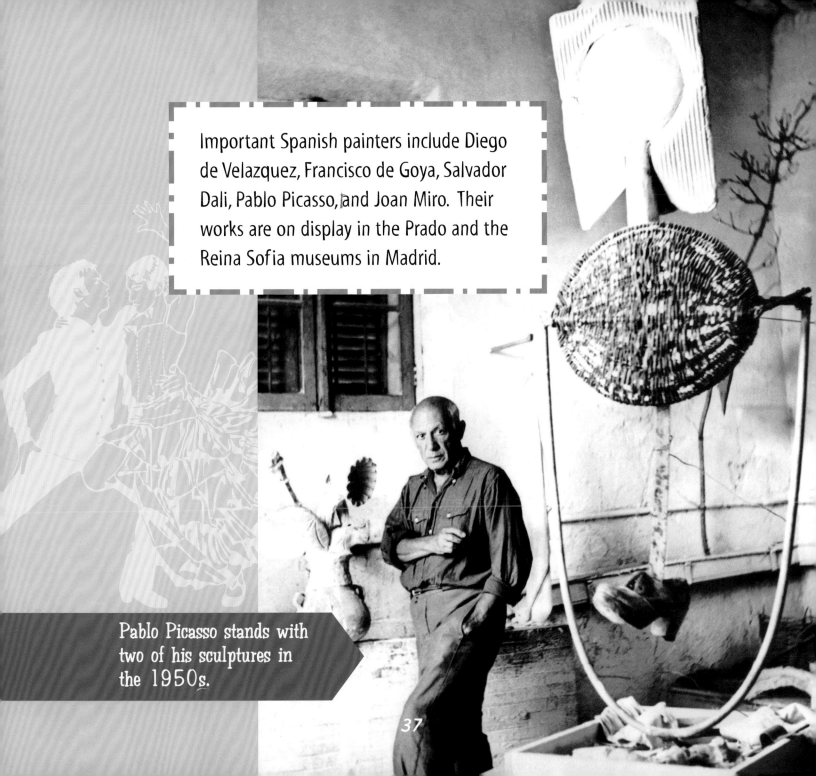

Important Spanish painters include Diego de Velazquez, Francisco de Goya, Salvador Dali, Pablo Picasso, and Joan Miro. Their works are on display in the Prado and the Reina Sofia museums in Madrid.

Pablo Picasso stands with two of his sculptures in the 1950s.

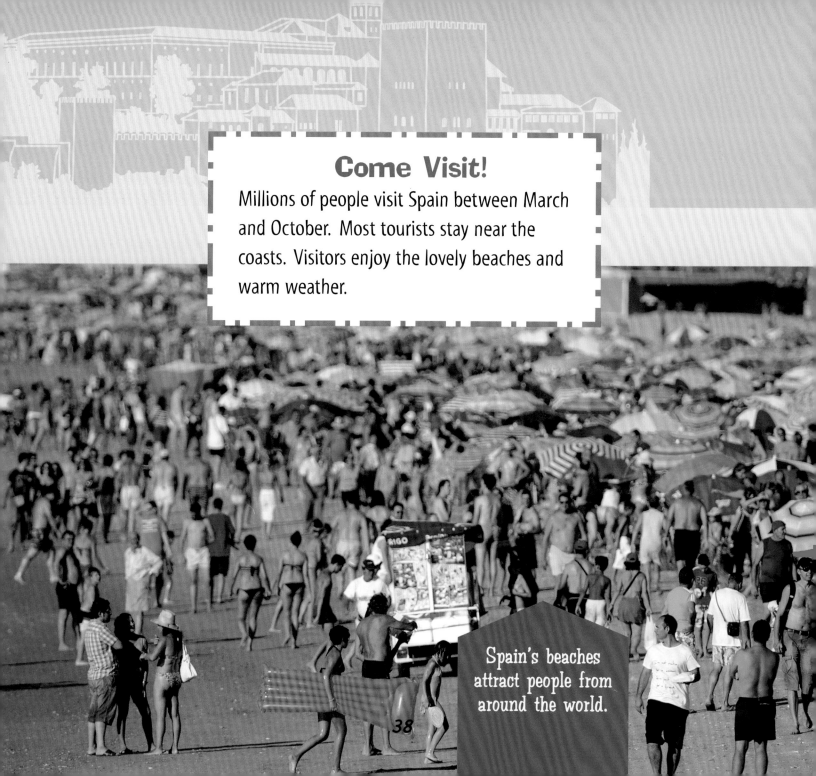

Come Visit!

Millions of people visit Spain between March and October. Most tourists stay near the coasts. Visitors enjoy the lovely beaches and warm weather.

Spain's beaches attract people from around the world.

Antonio Gaudi designed this park in Barcelona, including the curved benches these tourists are resting on.

Other tourists visit famous landmarks. These might include the Alhambra, a famous Moorish castle. Ancient Roman buildings bring tourists to Segovia and Merida. And the modern building style of Antonio Gaudi attracts visitors to Barcelona.

Schooling

Spanish children go to school from the ages of six to sixteen. Some kids start school before the age of six. Some go on to more studies after the age of sixteen.

Children in northern Spain listen to their teacher.

Kids study math, history, science, and Spanish. They have a lot of homework. It's a good thing dinner isn't until late. The kids have time to get their homework done before they eat!

These students are working on homework.

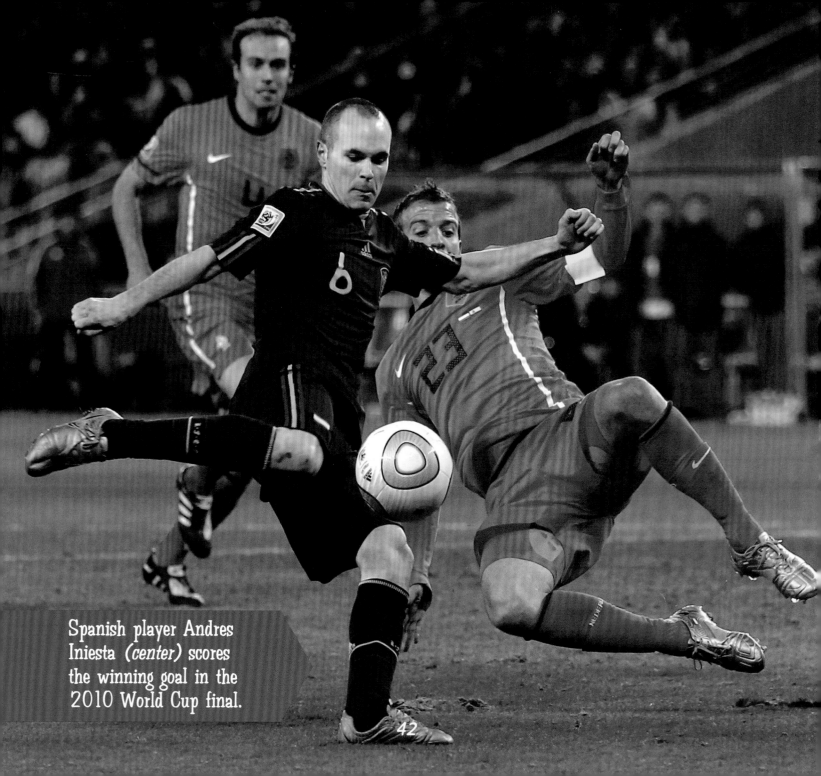

Spanish player Andres
Iniesta *(center)* scores
the winning goal in the
2010 World Cup final.

42

Score!

Soccer is the most popular sport in Spain. The national team won the World Cup in 2010. Then the entire country celebrated. Awesome!

Spain has won many Olympic gold medals in sailing and cycling. The country hosted the Summer Olympics in 1992.

Rafa

One of the most popular Spanish athletes is Rafael (Rafa) Nadal. This tennis player comes from the Balearic island of Mallorca. Rafa has won Olympic gold as well as many international tennis matches.

Rafael Nadal has won all the major tennis tournaments.

THE FLAG OF SPAIN

Three bands stretch across Spain's flag. The top and bottom bands are red. The wide middle band is yellow. Spain's coat of arms sits on this band. This flag was adopted in 1981.

FAST FACTS

FULL COUNTRY NAME: Kingdom of Spain

AREA: 195,363 square miles (505,988 square kilometers), or about twice the size of Wyoming

MAIN LANDFORMS: the coastal plain; the Meseta; the mountain ranges Cantabrian and Pyrenees; the Sierra de Guadarrama, the Sierra Morena, and the Sierra Nevada

MAJOR RIVERS: Ebro, Guadalquivir

ANIMALS AND THEIR HABITATS: brown bears, foxes, Iberian lynx, long-haired mountain goats, wolves (mountains); lizards, rabbits, snakes (Meseta); dolphins, jellyfish, whales (coasts)

CAPITAL CITY: Madrid

OFFICIAL LANGUAGE: Castilian Spanish

POPULATION: about 46,900,000

GLOSSARY

ancient: having been around for a long time, or very old

goods: things to sell

mainland: the main part of a country, separate from its islands

map: a drawing or chart of all or part of Earth or the sky

mountain: a part of Earth's surface that rises high into the sky

plateau: a high, flat area

port: an area on the shore of a body of water where ships can load and unload goods safely

saint: a holy man or woman honored by a village, a city, or a country

tourist: a person who visits a place on vacation

TO LEARN MORE

BOOKS

Grack, Rachel. *Spain*. Minneapolis: Bellwether Media, 2010. Learn more about Spain in this colorful book.

Greene, Jacqueline Dembar. *The Secret Shofar of Barcelona*. Minneapolis: Kar-Ben Publishing, 2009. Like other Jews in Spain in the 1500s, concert leader Don Fernando hides his Jewish faith. During a concert, he and his son Rafael come up with a way to celebrate the Jewish New Year by using the shofar, a ram's-horn instrument, in plain sight of Spanish Catholic leaders.

Lowery, Linda. *Pablo Picasso*. Minneapolis: Millbrook Press, 1999. This colorful biography showcases the life and work of the famous Spanish painter.

Sonneborn, Liz. *The Romans: Life in Ancient Rome*. Minneapolis: Millbrook Press, 2010. Fun artwork depicts the daily life, religion, ideas, and lasting influence of the ancient Roman Empire of which Spain was a part.

WEBSITES

Enchanted Learning
http://www.enchantedlearning.com/europe/spain/flag
This site has pages of Spain and its flag to label and color.

Time for Kids
http://www.timeforkids.com/TFK/teachers/aw/ns/main/0,28132,1534234,00.html
This general site has a section on Spain that includes a quiz, pictures, and a timeline.

INDEX

The images in this book are used with the permission of: © Martin Child/Digital Vision/Getty Images, p. 4; © Laura Westlund/Independent Picture Service, pp. 5, 44; © Luis Castaneda Inc./The Image Bank/Getty Images, pp. 6, 8; © Larry Mangino/The Image Works, p. 7; © Robert Harding Picture Library/SuperStock, p. 9; © David Sanger/The Image Bank/Getty Images, p. 10; © age fotostock/SuperStock, pp. 11, 15; © imagebroker.net/SuperStock, pp. 12, 27; © Bob Turner/Art Directors & TRIP, pp. 13, 31; © Josep Lago/AFP/Getty Images, p. 14; © Travel Library Limited/SuperStock, p. 16; © Stock Connection/SuperStock, p. 17; © Mary Evans Picture Library/The Image Works, p. 18; © Visual & Written/SuperStock, p. 19; AP Photo, pp. 20, 37; AP Photo/Paul White, p. 21; © Travel Ink/Gallo Images/Getty Images, pp. 22, 36; © Axiom Photographic Limited/SuperStock, p. 23; © JMN/Cover/Getty Images, p. 24; © Jasper Juinen/Getty Images, p. 25; © Chris Walsh/Photodisc/Getty Images, p. 26; © Radius Images/Getty Images, p. 28; © Martin Barraud/Stone/Getty Images, p. 29; © Jeremy Woodhouse/Photodisc/Getty Images, p. 30; © Dieter Telemans/Panos Pictures, p. 32; © Jochem D. Wijnands/The Image Bank/Getty Images, p. 33; © JTB Photo/SuperStock, p. 34; © Jupiterimages/FoodPix/Getty Images, p. 35; © Cristina Quicler/AFP/Getty Images, p. 38; © Murat Taner/Photographer's Choice/Getty Images, p. 39; © Cesar Manso/AFP/Getty Images, p. 40; © Siqui Sanchez/Flickr/Getty Images, p. 41; © Lars Baron/Getty Images, p. 42; AP Photo/Kathy Willens, p. 43.

Front cover: © Simeone Huber/Stone/Getty Images.

Main body text set in Myriad Tilt 17/22. Typeface provided by Adobe Systems.